Smell Science

Noxious Nature

Mary Gribbin

Illustrated by Peter Kavanagh

OXFORD
UNIVERSITY PRESS

Oxford University Press, Great Clarendon Street, Oxford OX2 6DP

Oxford New York
Athens Auckland Bangkok Bogotá Buenos Aires Calcutta
Cape Town Chennai Dar es Salaam Delhi Florence Hong Kong Istanbul
Karachi Kuala Lumpur Madrid Melbourne Mexico City Mumbai
Nairobi Paris São Paulo Singapore Taipei Tokyo Toronto Warsaw
and associated companies in Berlin Ibadan

Oxford is a registered trade mark of Oxford University Press

© Mary Gribbin 1999
The moral rights of the author have been asserted
First published 1999
The creator of the 'Smelly Science' series concept is Mary Dobson.

Cover artwork by Vince Reid.

British Library Cataloguing in Publication Data available

ISBN 0 19 910577 4

1 3 5 7 9 10 8 6 4 2

Printed in Great Britain

CONTENTS

SCIENCE MAKES SENSE. 4

THE SMELLY SUPER-HIGHWAY 6

DISGUSTING DEFENCES 8

HORRIBLE HUNTERS. 10

LOATHSOME LURES 12

TERRIBLE TABLE MANNERS 14

AROMATIC ATTRACTIONS. 16

POWERFUL PLANTS 18

LOATHSOME LODGINGS 20

PUTREFYING POISONERS AND AWFUL ANIMALS. 22

NOCTURNAL NASTIES. 24

NOXIOUS NATURE NOTES. 26

REVOLTING RAINFORESTS 28

PUTRID PUZZLES. 30

GLOSSARY. 31

INDEX 32

Scratch the scented panels lighly with a fingernail
to release their smell.

SCIENCE MAKES SENSE

Nature smells! Whether you're rambling through the rainforest, or tiptoing through the tulips, those pungent plants and aromatic animals certainly do get up your nose. But that's because being smelly can be useful. Smell can help them find food, detect danger, meet a mate and keep their young alive. What looks to us like their horrible habits is actually their very own information super-highway, whizzing mouldy messages as fast as you can send your friends an e-mail.

Using our powerful sense of smell is a wonderful way to get to grips with the creatures and features of the natural world. So sit tight for a revolting ramble through some truly terrible territory, using your sense of smell to make sense of noxious nature.

Of course, most other animals are much better at sniffing out smelly messages than we are. The smell zone inside your nose is less than 5 cm^2 — a sheep dog's is 116 cm^2, and a shark's is a terrifying 2230 cm^2 — so it can smell you coming long before you can smell, or even see, it!

Many creatures mark out their territory with scent — when your cat rubs itself lovingly against your legs, it's really only spreading its feline fumes on to you, from scent glands on the side of its head. Of course plants can't smell — but we can smell them alright. We love the delicious aroma of beautiful blooms, but there are some powerfully potent plants out there, if you know where to look. Read on for a sniff of the deadly and the disgusting, and remember:

Rose are red,
Violets are blue,
Nature is smelly —
And it's all really true!

THE SMELLY SUPER-HIGHWAY

Have you ever wondered why dogs don't just wee properly once, instead of sprinkling almost every tree and wall they pass? If you were a dog you'd understand, because dogs use scent like an invisible fence, so their wee is a handy, smelly KEEP OUT sign. It's a powerful message! Cats also use smell to mark out their territory. Male lions let everyone know where they want to be king by weeing on bushes and on the ground — so if you smell lion wee, watch out!

If you think taking your dog for a walk can be embarrassing, just be grateful you haven't been sent out with a male white rhinoceros! They like to mark out their territory with huge heaps of dung, which they kick around then top off with a powerful, stinking jet of wee — phew!

Animals don't use smells only to mark out their territory. It's also their information super-highway. They can learn a lot about each other by sniffing their stinking scent glands. That's why dogs sniff each other's bottoms — the anal gland just under their tails can say so much about their canine companions. A dog's sense of smell is so good, it can even tell if another dog is afraid just by its smell.

Smell was probably the first sense that animals developed all those millions of years ago. Early mammals were probably particularly pongy, because they were nocturnal (awake at night, asleep by day) and smell was the best way to communicate in the dark.

DISGUSTING DEFENCES

Animals need to drive away danger, and what better than a noxious whiff to keep their enemies at bay? Mostly they just want to be left in peace, but rub them up the wrong way and you'll be sorry! So always be kind to animals — and never, ever, annoy a skunk. An annoyed skunk will stamp its back paws to try to drive you away. But if you're silly enough to hang around teasing after that — beware the worst smell in the world!

The skunk's ultimate weapon is a fine spray of noxiously smelly yellow liquid, which it squirts from scent glands on either side of its bottom. This pongy jet is so powerful that it can travel almost 5 metres — and if it hits you it'll take weeks to get rid of the smell!

Scratch and sniff for a skunky whiff!

Like skunks, stonefish don't go out looking for trouble, they just want to be left alone on the sea bed. But step on one and — ouch, you're in for a truly poisonous punishment! Thirteen strong spiky spines on its back, each full of vile venom, rise up, push through your shoes and into your flesh. The venom shoots up into the wound, and your foot swells into an agonisingly painful ball.

The deadliest venom on earth belongs to the pretty little golden arrow frog, which is only 2-3 cm long. The gland under the skin of just one frog contains enough poison to kill almost 2,000 humans. People living in the rainforests of South America use this vicious venom on their darts when they go hunting.

The stink pot turtle of North America isn't very big either — but if hunted by a bird it lets off such a stupendous stink that its attacker soon lets go.

Even worms and beetles can get nasty if they feel threatened. Velvet worms in South America defend themselves by squirting a vile sticky liquid all over their attackers. Bombardier beetles are only just over 1 cm long, but if attacked they fire a noisy stream of noxious liquid chemicals out of their bottoms — in 500 bursts a second!

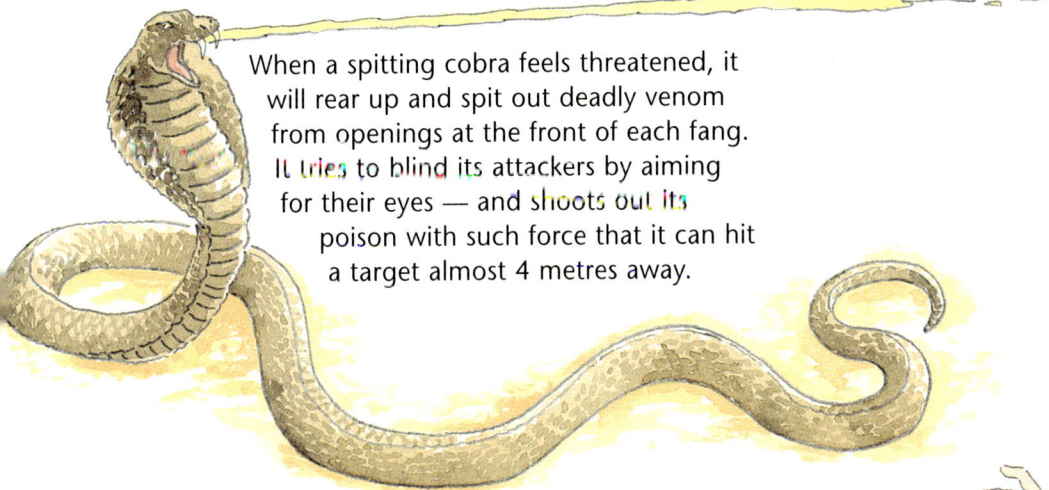

When a spitting cobra feels threatened, it will rear up and spit out deadly venom from openings at the front of each fang. It tries to blind its attackers by aiming for their eyes — and shoots out its poison with such force that it can hit a target almost 4 metres away.

Plants can't spit or run away, but stinging nettles have their own noxious form of self-defence. When you touch a nettle, the spiky hairs growing on the stems break your skin, injecting you with chemicals that cause a painful rash. So if you've grappled with nasty nettles once, you certainly won't try it twice!

Horrible Hunters

All living things need food to stay alive — and some have evolved disgusting ways of making sure they get it. Sleepy looking snakes, cute creepy crawlies — even some beautiful blooms — have putrid plans and revolting ruses to trap and kill their mealtime morsels.

The hanging pitcher plant eats flies! And it has a particularly nasty way of going about it. The insects are attracted to its brightly coloured flowers, which look a bit like a jug (or pitcher). But once they land on the rim of the flower they're doomed — it's so slippery that they slither into a putrid pool of juice. The biggest pitcher plant flowers can hold 2 litres of this foul fluid, which slowly digests any bodies that fall into it.

The imperial scorpion is seriously bad news if you're a lizard or a small invertebrate. It prefers to kill with its huge pincers, but if that doesn't work quickly, it will jab your squishy parts with the deadly, venomous sting at the end of its tail. Once the poison's done its worst, the scorpion's jaws can tear you apart slowly.

Tarantulas are everybody's scariest spider. They come in a frightening variety of sizes. The goliath tarantula is the largest spider in the world: up to 9 cm long, with a leg span of 26 cm — that's as big as your dinner plate! Their favourite dinner is small creatures and birds, which they strike with their hideous, powerful fangs. Spiders can only eat liquid food, so the venom they inject breaks down their victims' insides, leaving the soft squishy parts to be sucked up and digested. Yuk!

The giant scolopendra is nearly 30 cm long — and the biggest, vilest-looking centipede in the world. Centipedes don't all really have 100 legs. Some scolopendras only have 21 pairs of legs — which makes them less than fiftypedes! This horrible hunter has developed the front pair of legs, just behind its head, into poisonous claws which can kill a small creature with one nasty nip.

Even under the sea, creatures capture their dinners in hideous and disgusting ways. The yellow-lipped sea krait is a sea snake, which uses its brilliant sense of smell to seek out food. Once it catches an eel, it kills it with a line of venomous bites from its fangs all along the eel's body.

The cannibal chiasmodon fish has a belly hanging underneath it, like an enclosed life raft. As well as dining on other cannibal chiasmodon fish, it preys on sea creatures bigger than itself. After ripping them apart with its needle-sharp teeth, it stores the body bits in its expandable tum, to digest later when it's a bit peckish.

LOATHSOME LURES

The plants of noxious nature use the incredible power of smell to make sure they survive — by attracting insects to help them reproduce. Most flowers breed through pollination, when pollen from the male part of the flower is carried to the female part, so that fertilisation can happen and seeds can form. Plants can't move about, so many of them persuade insects to carry the pollen for them. And it isn't always the sweetest scent that brings in the creepy crawlies . . .

The stinking giant is the flower of the *Rafflesia arnoldii*. Each flower weighs more than 6 kg, making it the heaviest flower in the world, and it has some truly terrible habits. It must attract flies to pollinate the flowers. And what do flies like best? Rotting meat, of course! So the stinking giant lures them in by filling the air with a vile stink like rotting meat, which they find quite captivating.

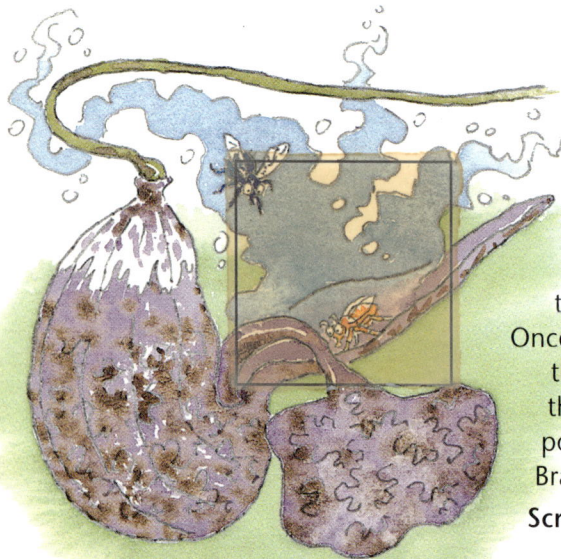

The Brazilian birthwort has a similarly brilliant trick. It entices flies by producing the alluring smell of long-dead fish. This irresistible odour entices the flies in through the narrow front of the flower. Once they're in, there's no way out until the flower withers and dies. By the time they can get out they're covered in pollen, so they fly off ready to help the Brazilian birthwort pollinate.

Scratch and sniff for a dead-fish whiff!

Animals also use smell to make sure they survive.
Deer, for example, have seriously sensitive noses and
attract their mates by leaving their alluring aromas
everywhere they pass. Some types have scent glands
between their toes — so they can leave fragrant
footprints! They also have them under their eyes, so
spread their amorous, smelly messages by rubbing
their faces on twigs and grasses.

Giant pandas love to be alone. To
warn off other pandas of the same sex
they rub their bottoms against the
trees they live among, leaving a whiffy
'keep away' message. But if they sniff
a panda whiff of the opposite sex —
they're off!

Terrible Table Manners

Has anyone ever told you off for not eating nicely? Noxious nature has plenty of creatures that grab their grub in nastier ways than even you can imagine.

Take the star fish. It uses its suckers to prise open a shellfish's shell just a few millimetres, then it squeezes its flobby stomach through the tiny crack, wraps it around the shellfish flesh and digests it slowly. The star fish then squeezes its tum out of the empty shell, and goes off looking for its next victim.

Vampire bats are the vilest predators. They fly out of their caves at night, sneak up on a nice, big, sleeping, warm-blooded animal — and sink their sharp, chisel-like teeth into its flesh. Slowly, they suck up its delicious blood. They have a handy trick of curling up their tongues like a drinking straw, to make the slurping that little bit easier. These vicious vampire bats are tiny — only about 9 cm long — but sometimes they drink so much blood they end up too fat to fly!

Did you think it would all be perfect manners under the sea? Wrong! Some foul fish live off the pests and dead skin of other fish. These 'cleaner fish' are welcomed by bigger sea creatures, who are happy to be tidied up by a fish wanting a take-away.   'Cleaner fish' can even nibble away safely down a shark's throat!

The banded coral shrimp is an undersea toothbrush. It swims right into the mouth of the enormous, ferocious moray eel, and eats up the leftover scraps stuck between its needle-sharp teeth. Very tasty!

Aromatic Attractions

Imagine a world without the wonderful smells of flowers and fruit! Nature isn't always noxious, and although we can't smell nearly as well as most animals, our sense of smell is a powerful friend in a fragrant world. We can detect a strong smell even if it makes up just 25 billionths of the air around us. Scratch and sniff below for a fragrant whiff

So no wonder we love the perfumed plants of the garden. But there's a pungent purpose behind the beautiful blooms of the lavender, rose and honeysuckle. The sumptuous smells lure pollinating insects, which carry the pollen from the male to the female parts of the flower. Result — a fertilising frenzy, producing seeds.

The seeds are often wrapped up in sweet-smelling fruits, to tempt animals and birds to eat them — delicious for the animal, and essential for the plants. The seeds of plums, cherries and raspberries return to the earth in the animal's poo — the best way to plant a new tree!

17

POWERFUL PLANTS

Everyone loves a fragrant garden — but not all plants are so pleasant, as you're about to find out.

The durian is one fruit that definitely doesn't smell sweet. It grows in the Philipinnes, Malaysia and Thailand, and would be a lot easier to eat if you had absolutely no sense of smell. The insides taste lovely, but you have to be brave to get that far. The spiky outside smells like a mixture of rotten onions and sewage. For a really putrid picnic, try eating a durian underneath a *Ocotea bulata* tree — also known as a stinkwood!

Strangler figs murder the trees they live on. Deep in the rainforest, they grow on the tops of the trees, to get at the light. Soon they send down roots, through the air and into the ground. As those roots grow big and strong, they twine around the trunk of the tree the strangler fig is living on, and slowly crush it to death - there's gratitude for you!

Ant plants also live high up on trees, but they make much better lodgers! Once firmly rooted, an ant plant develops a spiky, swollen stem which becomes home for a vast colony of ants. They get to build a complicated network of chambers where they can rear new ants and dump their droppings, and in return the ant plant gets food from their rubbish — sounds like a fair deal.

There's more than one reason not to go near the castor oil plant. Not only do its beans produce the revolting castor oil — they also contain one of the world's most powerful poisons, called ricin. Eating just one deadly bean would be enough to make you a 'has-been'!

Fancy taking home a souvenir from your seaside holiday? Don't try it in California, where the Giant Kelp seaweed can grow up to 200 metres long! It's the world's largest seaweed.

LOATHSOME LODGINGS

In the cut-throat world of nasty nature, animals and plants will do whatever it takes to survive — even if it means living in the most putrid, pongy places. Take a deep breath for a whiff of these horrible habitats.

Dung beetles live for dung! They spend most of their lives collecting dung and rolling it into neat little balls. Then the female lays her eggs in these and pushes them down into cosy underground egg chambers. The larvae soon hatch — and guess what they get for their very first meal? That's right — a tasty dollop of energy-packed dung!

Black burying beetles fly out after dark, searching for the bodies of small dead animals or birds. When they find one they dig away the earth from around it, to bury it. They lay their eggs on top of the grave — so that their newly-hatched baby beetles will have a lovely rotting corpse to eat.

Common brown rats find life on a rubbish tip putridly perfect. The rotting rubbish generates heat, which they love and which also attracts the slow-worms that make a handy rat snack. Brown rats also love life in the smelly sewers. They are expert swimmers and climbers, and love to scavenge their way through the pipes, ankle deep in filthy water.

House flies are horrible. Although they only live for about 20 days, they make the most of it, paddling in poo and revelling in rot. They turn any food they find into liquid, by spitting out their saliva all over it then sucking it up again. They can smell a piece of flesh 7 km away. So keep that food covered!

Nocturnal Nasties

You can often spot a nocturnal creature by its big eyes or ears, which pick up the faintest light or sound. But their most valuable sense is their sense of smell — how else could they find food in the dark?

Snakes detect smells with their Jacobson's organ, a tiny pit in the roof of their mouth. When they flick their tongues in and out they press its forked tip up into the Jacobson's organ to 'taste' the smell. This is really useful for hunting by night. Puff adders sniff out their dinner in the dark, and inject it with a deadly dose of venom. When the animal crawls off to die, the puff adder smells out the corpse.

Tuataras look like large lizards. They are genuinely prehistoric animals, looking much the same now as they did 200 million years ago. These repulsive reptiles live on islands off the coast of New Zealand, where they hunt insects at night.

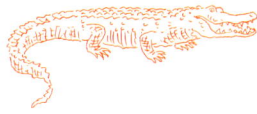

Noxious Nature Notes

Beastly babies
Baby cobras can bite animals and kill them with their venomous fangs as soon as they emerge from their eggs!

Fangs a lot
Gaboon vipers have the longest fangs of any snake in the world, and they produce the most venom. One pair of 10 cm long fangs contains more than 1000 mg of poison.

Fangs aloft
Pit vipers have a pair of heat sensitive pits between their eyes, to help them detect the warm bodies of their prey on dark nights. They can fold away their long fangs, up onto the roof of their mouth, when not in use — just like a loft ladder!

Sticky web
Gladiator spiders weave sticky webs, stretch them out between their legs, and then drop the outstretched web down on top of passing insects to trap them.

Electric cookers
Atlantic torpedo ray fish have an electrifying way of killing their food. They zap their prey with a 225 volt electric shock — enough electricity to knock out a human — then gobble it up.

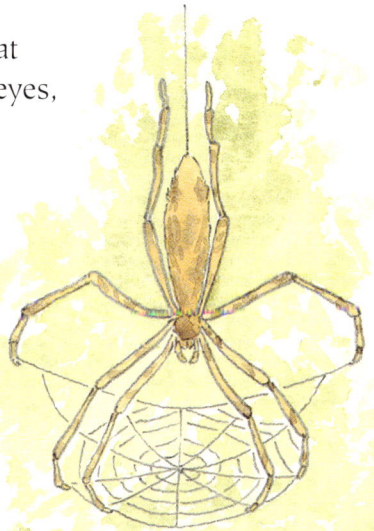

Fruit bats love — fruit! Huge colonies of them sleep by day in shadowy, dark caves. At night they swoop out and head for the fruit plantations. These fussy eaters only like the juiciest bits — the rest is spat out. Their disgusting devastation can destroy a fruit farm in one night. There are over 150 different kinds of fruit bat. One of them, the flying fox, has a wingspan of 1.5 metres!

Owls swoop down silently on little rodents and swallow them whole. They digest all the soft fleshy bits, and make the hard bones into pellets, which they cough up and spit out.

The nocturnal cat-eyed snake will only eat frogs' eggs. It is so brilliant at finding them, that frogs in the rainforest can only survive by laying so many eggs that some escape the snake's greedy glances.

Geckos are nocturnal lizards that run about at night hunting insects. They have pads on their toes covered with tiny bristles that hook on to any surface they are running over — so they can run up walls and across ceilings even on the darkest night.

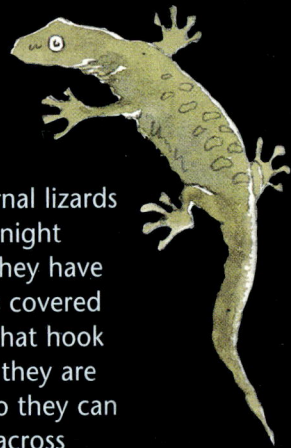

Most people think hyenas only pick over the food that lions leave behind. They do this by day, but at night they become horrible hunters themselves, in packs of 30 or more. Sometimes lions even eat their leftovers!

A TIGHT SQUEEZE

Boa constrictors pick up the scent of passing creatures through sensors in their tongues and on the roof of their mouths. They then strike with their fangs, before crushing the creature to death by coiling themselves tighter and tighter around it.

KICK ME QUICK

Cassowarys are killer birds. Although they can't fly, they have a kick powerful enough to kill, and a temper so quick that they will attack anyone who comes too close!

DON'T BE DUMB

The leaves of the dumb cane plant are full of poisonous sap. If you eat one, your mouth will swell up so much that you won't be able to talk.

TASTY TRAP

The venus fly trap is a meat-eating plant! Its leaf is split into two halves, joined by a leafy hinge to make a terrible trap. When an insect lands on the leaf, the trap springs shut! The insect is crushed to death and dissolved into a mushy mess by chemicals inside the leaf.

VILE VOMIT

Annoy a camel and it will sick up part of the foul food in its stomach — and spit it in your eye!

REVOLTING RAINFORESTS

More than three quarters of all the plants and animals on Earth live in rainforests — that's 60,000,000 different species. Rainforests are hot, wet jungles, where everything grows thick and fast. Up in the canopy at the top of the trees it is sunny and light. But under the treetops is the shadowy understorey, and down on the ground it is cool and dark. But wherever you look, it's teeming with creepy creatures . . .

Danger even lurks up in the sky. Philippine eagles soar over the treetops, their eagle eyes spotting the prey which they swoop down on and rip apart with their razor-sharp hooked beaks.

Flying lizards in the rainforests of South East Asia flatten their ribs out on either side of their bodies, so they look like Concord. They then leap into the air and can glide for 15 metres or more.

In the Amazon rainforest even fish can fly! Hatchet fish can glide more than 5 metres above the water.

Even the river isn't safe. Some types of piranha fish swim in shoals that can devour an animal in minutes.

PUTRID PUZZLES

1. Which of these animals would take you for the smelliest walk?
a) a sheep
b) a male white rhinoceros
c) a hamster

2. How do pitcher plants eat flies?
a) covered in ketchup
b) in a toasted sandwich
c) by digesting them in a foul fluid

3. Which of these plants produces the foulest fragrance?
a) strangling fig
b) stinking giant
c) rose

Awful anagrams

Rearrange these letters to make:

A plant that smells of dead fish   **NAILIZRAB THROWBIRT**

A spider as big as a dinner plate   **THOGALI RATANTLUA**

A fish with an expandable stomach   **NIBCANAL SIAMCHODON**

Hoatzin birds won't rip you apart, but they smell terrible. They eat so many leaves that they just rot inside their stomach — making them smell like feathered cow dung.
Scratch and sniff for a mouldy whiff.

Beware the 'corpse flower'! The flowers of the titan arum plant only live for a day, so they need a pretty powerful smell to attract flies to pollinate them. Believe it or not, the flies flock to its stench of rotting flesh — delicious!

Army ants live in gigantic colonies and march across the floor, killing any insects in their way. Their powerful jaws can rip apart any carcass they find. South American Indians use them to help heal wounds — one bite on either side of a gaping cut pulls the skin together like a stitch!

The stinkhorn fungus breeds by making spores that need to be spread around. Flies are perfect for this job, so the stinkhorn fungus makes a putrid potion, smelling like rotting meat, to lure them in.

Beneath the floor lives the red giant earthworm, almost 1 metre long.

INDEX

ant plant *19*
anteater *23*
ants *19, 23, 28*

bats *14, 25*
beetles *9, 20, 21*
Brazilian birthwort *12*
bush baby *23*

camel *27*
cassowary 27
castor oil plant *19*
cats *5, 6*
centipedes *11*
communication *4, 6-7, 13, 23*
corpse flower *28*

deer 13
defence *8-9*
dogs *6, 7*
dumb cane plant 27

eagle *29*

fish *8, 11, 14, 15, 26, 29*
flies *10, 12, 21, 28, 29*
flowers *4, 5, 10, 12, 16, 28*
frogs *9, 25*
fruit *16, 17, 18, 25*
fungus *29*

habitats *4, 9, 18, 20-21, 28-29*
hoatzin *29*

hunting *4, 9, 10-11, 14, 21, 22, 24, 25, 26, 27, 29*
hyena *25*

lizards *22, 24, 25, 28*

octopus *22*
owl *25*

panda *13*
pitcher plant *10*
poisons *8, 9, 10, 11, 19, 22, 4, 26, 27*
pollination *12, 17, 29*

rainforest *4, 9, 18, 28-29*
rats *21*
reproduction *4, 12, 13, 17, 28*
rhinoceros *6*

scent glands *5, 7, 8, 13*
seaweed *19*
shark *5*
skunk *8*
snakes *9, 10, 11, 24, 25, 26, 27*
spiders *10, 11, 22, 26*
stinging nettles *9*
strangler fig *18*

trees 18, 28
turtle *9*

venus fly-trap *27*

worms *9, 21, 28*

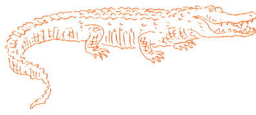

Glossary

colony   a large group of living creatures or plants living together in the same place.

fang   a long tooth. Some snakes inject poison into their prey through long hollow fangs.

fertilisation   the joining of the male and female reproductive cells.

invertebrate   an animal with no backbone.

larva   the stage in the lifecycle of a creature between hatching and becoming an adult.

Tadpoles and caterpillars are both larvae.

nocturnal   being active during the night and asleep by day.

pollination   the transfer of pollen from the male part of a flower to the female part, or from one plant to another.

predator   a creature that lives by hunting and eating other creatures.

prey   a creature that is hunted and eaten by another creature.

sap   the juice inside plants that carries food and water.

scent gland   a small organ in a creature's body that produces a strong smelling substance.

shoal   a large group of fish swimming together.

venom   poison